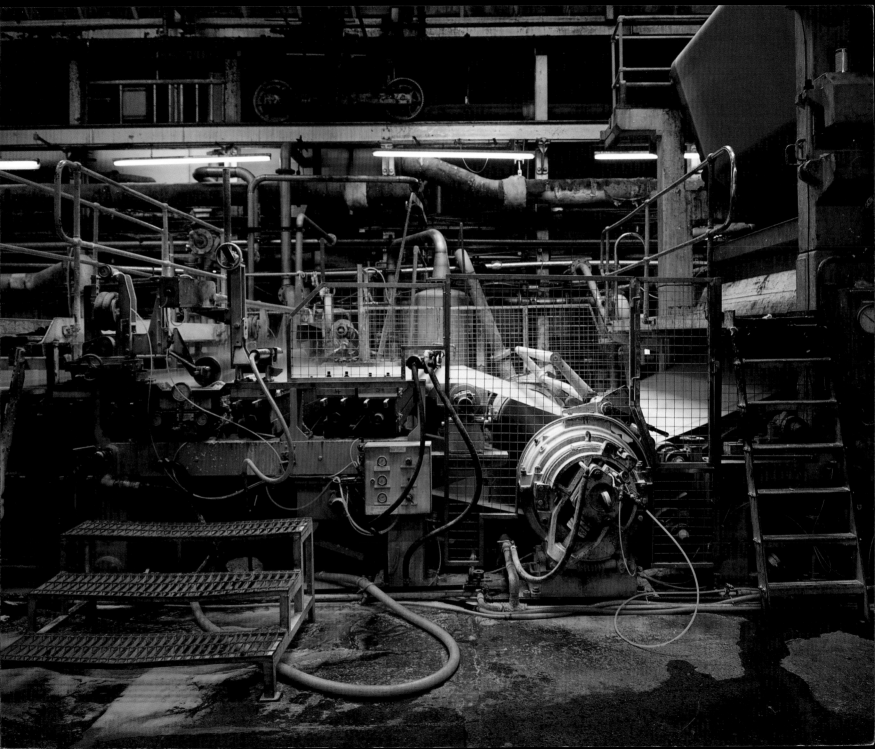

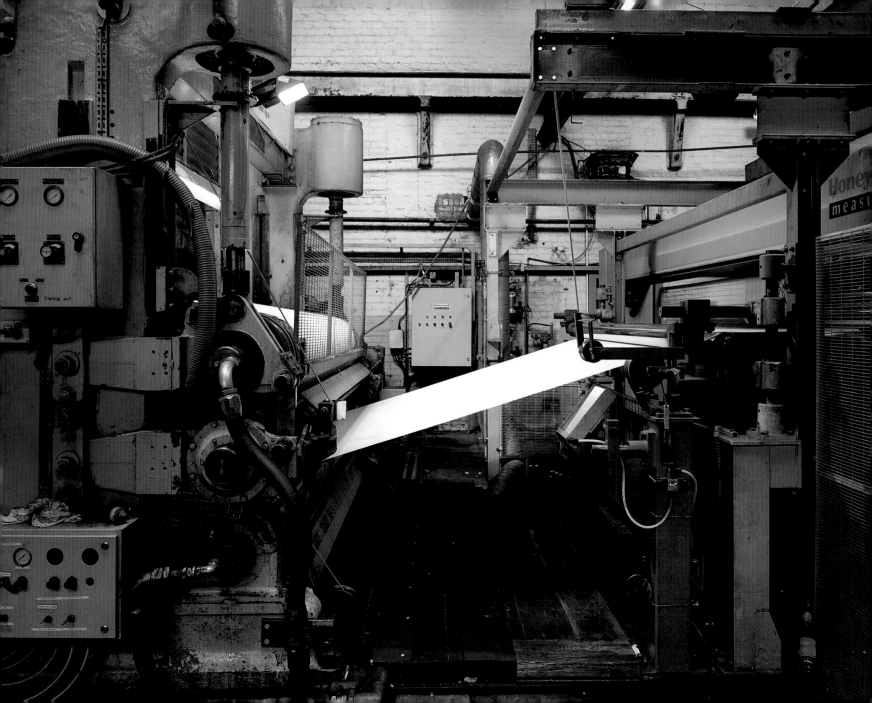

Simon Starling Djungel

Dundee Contemporary Arts
2002

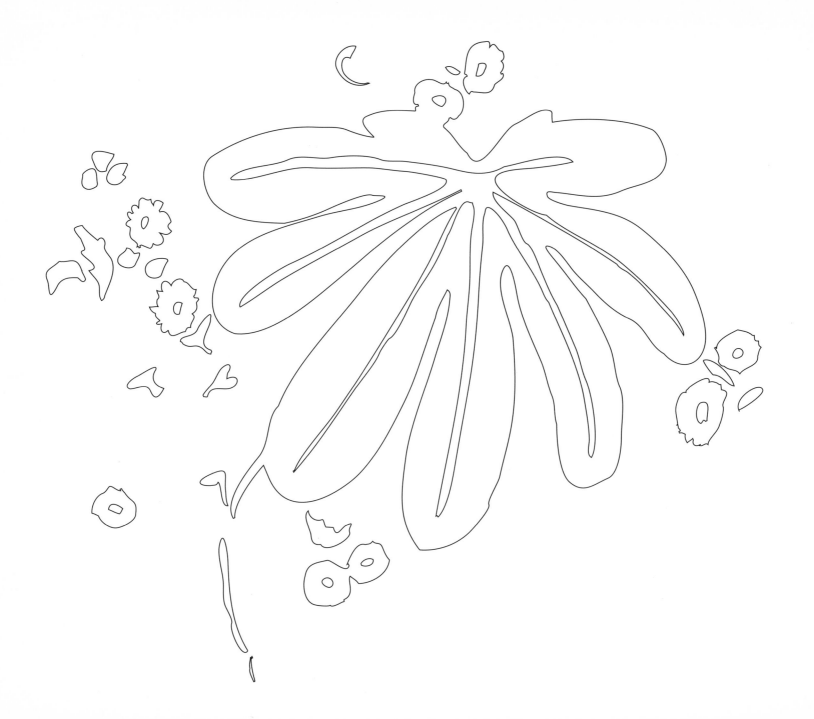

Laser drawings created by Simon
Starling and Ferranti Photonics after
Josef Frank's 'Aralia' c.1928.

Djungel Dwelling

KATRINA M. BROWN

Despite his own personal verdict on the significance of his achievements to the contrary, Johann Wolfgang von Goethe[1] is nowadays known primarily as a poet and playwright rather than a scientist. Yet his theories of science, or rather his suggested *way* of science – for he saw it as necessarily participatory, engaged and imaginative, rather than cerebral and rational – was an extraordinary vision, not only for its time, when the bases of so much modern science were being established, but also in terms of its increasing relevance to current discourses on relations between human beings and nature. Goethe's quest was for a kind of phenomenology that sought an awareness of the observer and the observed at one and the same time, a way of thinking that seems remarkably current today. In brief, Goethe sought what we might now call a holistic method, one which would allow all constituent parts of the chosen object of study to be kept present in the mind of the observer at the same time:

> If I look at the created object, inquire into its creation, and follow this process back as far as I can, I will find a series of steps. Since these are not actually seen together before me, I must visualise them in my memory so that they form a certain ideal whole. At first I will tend to think in terms of steps, yet nature leaves no gaps, and thus, in the end, I will have to see this progression of uninterrupted activity as a whole. I can do so by dissolving the particular without destroying the impression itself.[2]

Such an imaginative vision of the disparate, progressive steps in the development of a form is a fitting analogy for the way in which one encounters any of Simon Starling's large-scale projects. The approach he takes to his own chosen objects can be seen to exemplify Goethe's ideal way, though his focus is our material culture rather than the realm of nature. His approach shares with Goethe's a pursuit of knowledge THROUGH PRACTICE and a valuing – and enjoyment – of primary experience. He does not simply observe, he participates in the coming into being of the object.

These projects bring diverse sources and elements together in configurations which undermine the latent hierarchy – of object over process, end-product over source material, design over craft. They are synthetic rather than analytic, with each present, tangible and concrete element insisting on an awareness of the disparate histories and journeys necessary to the creation of the whole.

1. Johann Wolfgang von Goethe (German, b.1749 – d.1832) poet, playwright and scientist.

2. Goethe, *Scientific Studies*, quoted in 'Goethe's Way of Science: A Phenomenology of Nature', eds. D. Seamon and A. Zajonc (1998, State University of New York), p.133

Whatever the specific technical activity he engages in, there persists something of the amateur about Starling; the self-taught experimental scientist guided as much by feeling, intuition, instinct, visual stimuli and a not inconsiderable degree of pleasure. For the projects he has realised over the past five or six years he has proved himself extraordinarily rigorous and adaptable, teaching himself boat building, model aircraft construction, wood-block printing, aluminium production, chair manufacture and more. He has also travelled like a voracious eighteenth-century explorer, in search of the often obscure source of his objects. Like Goethe's near contemporary and one of the founders of modern geography, Alexander von Humboldt,[3] he has travelled between Western Europe and Central and Southern America: Surinam, Ecuador, Trinidad, Puerto Rico, southern Spain, Romania, France and Poland all feature in the recipes for his projects, the frequently extensive lists of ingredients that go into the mix of any one piece. He has traced histories back to the innovators, the originators and leaders in their field, those who established the way forward. The evocative interweaving of diverse people, places, objects and histories that is the recurrent pattern for his work tends to coalesce around the creation of a specific product. But whatever the technique he requires to adopt in order to realise his chosen product, the results always betray their hand-made genesis. Though they never fail in their intended function – you can sit on the chairs, fly the planes – neither do they achieve the full machine-finished form of the real thing. Crucially, it is these production values that, as Starling himself has said, 'allow people to immerse themselves in these fragile stories'.

The origins of many of these stories as encountered in any one piece are often to be found in previous works, with a number of long-running strands, which meet with enthusiastic interests in places, individuals and objects, variously intertwined with sporadic fascinations and intrigues. Some of these are celebratory and engaging, others critical and problematising, but all are associative and inclined to highlight the extraordinary complexities that can lie behind the most familiar domestic objects. To approach an appreciation of Starling's most recent work, it is worth recalling the genesis of a number of specific earlier pieces.

Invited to realise a new work for an exhibition at the Museum of Modern Art at Heide near Melbourne, in 1998 Starling started on one of his most ambitious projects to date. It brought together two key strands that permeate his most recent work, both of which are alluded to in the title of the piece: *Le Jardin suspendu*, the term given to the flat-roof gardens to be found in many a Modernist building. The first of these is the design and architecture of the Modern Movement and its trans-national spread via International Style. The Museum in which Starling was to exhibit was housed in lush parkland, rich with

3. Alexander von Humboldt (German, b.1769 – d.1859) naturalist and explorer

Le Jardin suspendu 1998   Installation view, Museum of Modern Art at Heide, Melbourne

a number of species imported from Europe. The parkland also housed a delightful modernist villa designed for its owners in 1965 by David McGlashan and Neil Everist, two Australian architects. The villa exemplified for Starling both the global spread of the International Style and its decorative exploitation of greenery – whether pre-existing or specifically planted – as a key element in villa design. A prominent feature of so much domestic architecture of the Modern Movement was of course the way in which it sought to unify interior and exterior, to bring the garden into the living space. Floor to ceiling picture windows looking out onto lush greenery are one of the signatures of the Modernist project – and worked wonderfully for the secluded villas of its most eminent patrons.

Struck by the distances travelled, the transportation of ideas, people and materials that lay behind the appearance of such a building in such a place, Starling looked to that most utterly modern invention – flight.

Le Jardin suspendu 1998
production still

He set about building a model airplane to be flown in the garden of the museum. He, of course, did not build a generic plane, but chose the specific design of a Farman 'Mosquito', which had been illustrated in Le Corbusier's famous *Towards a New Architecture*[4] in support of his argument that houses must be designed as 'machines for living in', just as planes were machines for flying in, designed to satisfy particular and clearly expressed needs.

4. Le Corbusier, *Vers une Architecture*, first published in 1923. *Towards a New Architecture*, Architectural Press, London, 1974.

The second prominent strand to appear in this work is an interest in plant life and the commercial uses of natural resources. Prompted partly by the (imported) museum parkland, partly by the Aboriginal tradition of creating transport (in their case canoes) from trees, and finally by the traditional materials of the model-maker, Starling decided to acquire a balsa wood tree, from which he would make the model aircraft. Typical of his on-going incorporation of the sources and origins of products and materials, Starling travelled to Ecuador to negotiate the acquisition of an appropriate tree, which was then shipped in part to his studio in Glasgow and in part to Heide. Balancing the intrinsically urban, rational and mechanical modernism of the 1920s plane (and its association with the best-known of the Modern movement's architects) with an essential, natural and rural source provides the fundamental tension to the resultant work.

The plane was flown in the garden, then shown in the museum, as it has been subsequently elsewhere, on a glass-topped table, with the remnants of the making of the model – including the remains of the tree – placed beneath it. Once removed from Heide, this set up has been accompanied by a large 'back-drop' of an image of the gardens, acknowledging the removals and shifts at play, a foretaste of a recurrent element in works to follow. A similar use of 'nature as backdrop' recurs in a number of Starling's most recent projects, in particular the vast project for the 'Djungel' exhibition at DCA, *Blue, Red, Green, Yellow, Djungel* (see below).

H.C. / H.G.W. 1999

Installation view Galerie
für Zeitgenössische Kunst,
Leipzig.

5. Charles Francis Annesley
Voysey (English, b.1857 –
d.1941) architect and
designer of fabrics,
wallpapers and furniture
associated with the English
Arts & Crafts movement,
whose best known exponent
was William Morris, which
promoted both a truth to
materials and an increased
simplicity of form.

The following year Starling produced a work in Leipzig that demonstrates similar fields of interest while also fore-grounding a relationship to site that is central to so many of his works. The Galerie für Zeitgenössische Kunst is housed in a three-storey villa designed for its geologist owner, Hermann Credner, in 1892. The elegant villa / gallery is positioned rather oddly, at an angle to the rectilinear street corner on which it stands, the reason for this being the presence of a large oak tree Credner did not want to have cut down to make way for his new home. So the house was built in deference to the tree, which much later, however, had to be cut down. Its trunk was nonetheless kept in the gardens of what was by then the gallery.

Starling used a piece of wood from this trunk to re-create a chair designed in England around 1885 by C. F. A. Voysey[5] – a 'swan chair', a design which, like several of those which have featured in Starling's recent work, takes its inspiration from nature. The chair – a close contemporary of the villa – takes the graceful line of a swan's neck as the elegant form of its sides, while its seat and back are of simple, straight wooden struts, which would have been covered by a canvas sling.

right **Home-made Eames (formers, jigs, moulds)** 2001

H.C. / H.G.W. (1999) presented the chair, still held in place by clamps and on the work sheet on which it had been formed, angled casually by one of the villa windows. It typifies a pre-Modernist, Arts and Crafts tradition of simple forms, truth to materials and use of imagery from the natural world. Making the chair for this villa-turned-gallery, Starling effectively creates at least two imaginative liaisons. The first between Voysey, whose architectural work is said to have been the basis for much small-scale 20th-century suburban housing, and Credner, contemporaries, possibly with shared ideas, who never met. The other, in the title, by referencing H. C. (Credner) and the English author, H. G. Wells, who was later to commission Voysey to design a house.[6]

6. H.G. Wells (English, b.1866 – d.1946) novelist, journalist, sociologist and explorer but best known as one of the first science fiction writers. His commission of Voysey was made possible by the profits generated by the success of his first major novel '*The Time Machine*', published in 1895.

With these two projects, *H.C. / H.G.W.* and *Le Jardin suspendu*, Starling had clearly developed his previous interest in the meaning and values of objects to a more focussed interest in the shaping of design history and our often problematic relationship with the natural world, with an empathy for the sites in which he works and an awareness of the individual personalities and labour behind what has become our material culture. Both works, like many that have followed, allow and encourage an enjoyment of the forms devised in the past (the plane and the chair). They prompt an appreciation of the admirable imagination, determination and effort that brought them into being, while never losing sight of the complex networks of economic, social and cultural conditions that were the context for their creation. Crucially they both also maintain a tangible manifestation of the labour-intensive process undergone by Starling to make them, bringing the oft neglected role played by nature into the equation of the resultant objects' worth.

Whatever the supposed differences in the principles of late nineteenth-century design such as Voysey's and the modernist work of subsequent figures such as Corbusier (the truth to materials and value of hand-craft versus industrialised mass production), their similarities are stronger – most markedly in the desire to simplify, to strip back unnecessary decoration and to improve living conditions. They are both symptomatic of the belief that if the world is to be any different (and hopefully better) if will have to *look* different. Starling's engagement with these objects and the histories behind them is not rooted purely in the aesthetic objective but, as he has said himself, 'Modernism is for me as much about social and economic change as it is about aesthetics. The aesthetic changes often came on the back of a desire for fundamental social change, they mimic this desire in some sense. It is about a move towards clarity, stripping away the façade.'[7]

7. See 'Simon Starling', Galerie für Zeitgenössische Kunst, Leipzig, 1999.

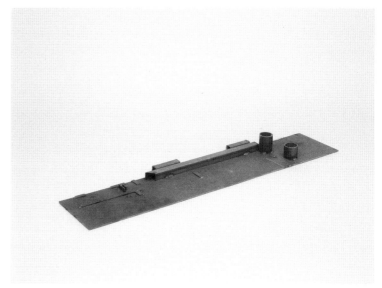

8 . Charles and Ray Eames (American; Charles b.1907 – d.1978; Ray b.1912 – d.1988)

9. From when it first came into production until 1993 the chair seat was made of fibreglass. In 1993, however, Vitra, the chair's manufacturers since 1984, discontinued production for ecological reasons, as fibreglass cannot be recycled. They have recently relaunched it with a polypropylene seat. See www.vitra.com

Perhaps the most renowned, remarkable and best-loved designers broadly associated with this social and economic impetus, the desire to improve living conditions for the masses are Charles and Ray Eames.[8] The Eames classic 'DSS' chair, designed in the immediate post-war period in 1948 was the first industrially-manufactured plastic chair[9]. These icons of Modernist design, once symbolic of new democratising forces, have been the focus for a number of Starling's projects. Now available at price to the few rather than the many, they have instead become indicative of wealth, taste and cosmopolitan flair, the revolutionary and socially conscious aspirations with which they were once invested almost entirely lost. *Home-made Eames (formers, jigs and moulds)* is a series of photographs in which Starling attempts to let us see these chairs through the eyes of their original makers. He made a number of replica chairs from scratch and the photographs show the various improvised tools and devices he had to create in order to do so – these are not the familiar forms of the chair itself but the negative forms and supports that helped bring it into being. The final form is legible in some of them – especially the mould for the distinctive seat – but largely what they convey is the experimental, hands-on, dirty material process of making something – a something that was to become the epitome of slick, clean and machine-finished design.

While Starling's approach to chair manufacture is in some respect analytical – submitting the object first to deconstruction to reveal the component parts and stages – his presentations tend to keep each stage present, keeping our eyes on the whole rather than the part. This was certainly the approach he took to an ambitious and typically idiosyncratic project made in Montpellier in 2001, in which commercial printing was similarly scrutinized. CMYK / RGB took the gallery's own current operational network as a starting point. For reasons of economy, the gallery's printed material is produced by a company in Cluj in Romania. Determined to make this unlikely connection visible, Starling travelled to Cluj to photograph the print workshop, housed in a former synagogue, which it shares with a TV studio. The images were to form the basis of a publication, which unlike normal exhibition catalogues, was to become both subject and product of the exhibition.

Replicating the divide found in the former synagogue, Starling created two spaces within the gallery. One contains neat stacks of printed images; of the route from the airport to the print workshop, the streets bedecked with the national colours of Romania (red, yellow and blue) and of the printing process in action. These untrimmed printed sheets await collation and binding to become the book. The second space houses a four-colour printing press that throughout the period of the exhibition runs off the sheets that will become the cover of the publication. The sheets bear an image of coloured light-bulbs and bunting – a detail from a heavily decorated street. Connecting the viewer back to her /

his own route to this point, the image was taken immediately outside the gallery in Montpellier, where Starling, parodying the surfeit of nationalist colour he found in Cluj, had installed CMYK (cyan, magenta, yellow, black) coloured bunting and RGB (red, green and blue) lights. Fusing three types of colour scheme, Starling's project brings their rationale and associations into question: the CMYK of four-colour printing and the RGB of television (to be found at work in the distant Romanian building) that lend the work its title; and the more emotive resonance of a national flag. The circular structure of the show / book thus juxtaposes and exposes diverse codes, making a visual connection between the specific and powerful local meaning of one system and the universal application of others.

Flaga (1972–2000) 2002

A piece first exhibited in Turin in 2002 demonstrates a similar exposure of the economic forces behind industrialised production. *Flaga (1972–2000)* brings to light the fact that the quintessentially Italian Fiat 126 was at one time manufactured in Poland, where cheaper labour and materials allowed for more cost-effective production. Starling took a red 126 bought in Turin, one of the last to be manufactured there before the transfer of production to Poland. He then drove it to the Polish site of their manufacture, replicating the economically-motivated geographic shift that occurred. There he bought body parts from a post-1973 Polish model and had them substituted for the originals on the red version. He then drove the hybrid car – now red and white – back to Turin, where it was hoisted onto the gallery wall. Its title taken from the Polish for 'flag', the Polish flag being, of course, red and white. *Flaga (1972–2000)* neatly encapsulates the coming together of two countries and demarcates a period of time from the car's first appearance to its withdrawal from the market in 2000. It is redolent with notions of national identity and pride and the

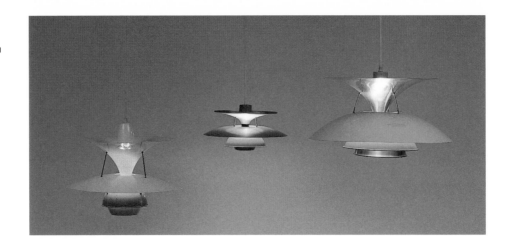

function of manufacture and industry as key components in that. If a country does not produce, from where does it garner its worth?

Such characteristic sensitivity to site, interest in the vernacular and a straightforward enjoyment of fabricating are similarly manifest is the series of cobbled-together lamp-shades entitled *Home-made Henningsen*. Begun in 2001, these objects (there are currently fifteen) are made from various metal lampshades and other items (such as a wok lid) found discarded or in second-hand shops by Starling in different places he visits. The re-sultant lamps may, therefore somehow portray the tastes of the inhabitants of the various locations from which they are culled. They emulate the designs of Poul Henningsen,[10] who sought with his revolutionary aluminium lamps to create a warmer and more diffuse quality of light than had previously been possible with electric lamps. His 'Paris Lamps' begun in the 1920s have become another design classic, but despite his belief that 'It doesn't cost money to light a room correctly, but it does require culture' the lamps are now priced beyond the reach of all but the wealthy. Henningsen's intentions were, like so many of his peers and foreign counterparts both honourable and socially minded:

It has always been the idea that the ph-lamp should be the lamp for the home. Due to its qualities and its modern appearance it had to be accepted first in offices and public buildings, but it is constructed with the most difficult and noble task in mind: lighting in the home. The aim is to beautify the home and those who live there, to make the evening restful and relaxing.

Lofty goals indeed but the intervention of corporate capitalism is accepted as a conduit to successful and, crucially, cost-effective production. Yet that same infra-structure can take an innocent object into a political and social hierarchy from which it and its designers find it difficult to escape. Starling's home made lamps, like the *Home-made Eames* chairs and several other works, foreground the essential relationship between scarcity and desirability that underscores demand in a market economy: once demand is established, limit the supply and you can increase the price. They similarly bring to mind issues about craft and labour, not dissimilar to those raised in earlier works by Mike Kelley and others: how and why some objects accrue value and others do not. The assumption of value or its absence in the hand-made truly questions the stated intent of democratising design – of making the functional and the stylish affordable. For Starling's lamps perform the same function and adhere to the same forms as the Henningsen originals: what they lack is the machine-made finish and the stamp of the (revered and professional) author. They are not 'authentic' Henningsen, their value therefore lessened – although ironically of course that may well ultimately be inverted by their eventual valuation as Simon Starling unique artworks.

The home-made quality of these and other Starling productions renders transparent the processes, perhaps even allowing the forms of desirable objects to be really seen for the first time, rather than merely recognised. The experiential shift is akin to that between knowledge and understanding. These questions recur through several of Starling's works,

from the series
Home-made Henningsen
2001

33

not least of which those with a museological slant. His *Blue Boat Black* (1997) for example – a small fishing boat constructed from the wood of a disused museum vitrine and then burnt to fuel the fire over which the fish caught from the boat were cooked – or more recently *The Pink Museum, Porto* in 2001. The starting point for this work was the realisation that three buildings in the city shared the same colour – a very specific 'Art Deco' pink, often seen on buildings of the 1920s or '30s (think Miami). The buildings were the Fundaçao Serralves (where the exhibition was to be held), a photographic studio and the ethnographic museum, which housed a particularly potent collection of artefacts, put together as it had been by soldiers bringing objects back from the colonies. Most of the objects are from Angola, providing a very tangible sense of Portugal's prior imperial power. Starling produced a series of fourteen photographs, eleven of objects from the museum collection against a backdrop of the same pink as the buildings in question and three

from **The Pink Museum, Porto** 2001

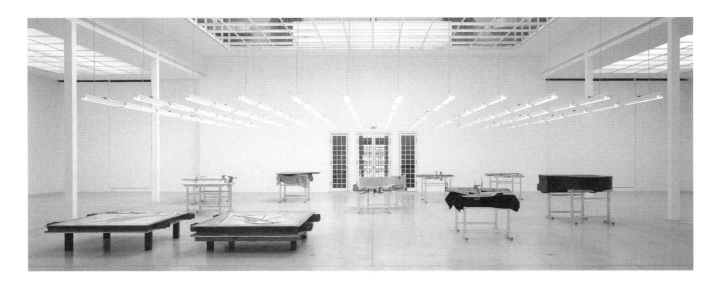

of the specific sites referenced and connected by the colour. The objects included a wicker bowl, a machine gun and a rather spindly potted plant.

The Pink Museum, Porto is, perhaps surprisingly, the first time Starling worked directly with a museum collection and as such it accentuates more than most his examination of the role of culture in the illustration of histories, how it is made evident in material form and how those histories are then depicted via museum displays. It also revives the notion of the museum as a place of subjective pleasure and wonder, with objects selected through personal fascination and intrigue, rather than scientific, objective analysis.

Like so many of his works, *The Pink Museum, Porto* highlights the fuzzy or even absent logic that lies at the root of so many received and accepted structures (why *that* pink?) at play in our culture. It also returns us to the often idiosyncratic and eccentric origins of so many museum collections that were rooted in the personal passions and enthusiasms of individuals. It gives preference to visual pleasure over education and history telling. Starling seeks out the intuitive and the unexpected, the invisible substratae. From the ethnography collection he moved on to the high culture of modern classical music and the grand piano for another ambitious work realised for the Secession in Vienna. *Inverted Retrograde Theme* (2001) rendered physical and visible an innovative method of musical composition invented by one of the city's many famous sons, Arnold Schoenberg.[11] His 'twelve-tone' method of composition broke with the traditional system of tonal organisation that had

Inverted Retrograde Theme
2001

Installation view Secession, Vienna

11. Arnold Schoenberg (Austrian, b.1874, Vienna – d. 1951, Los Angeles), Jewish-born composer who emigrated to the U.S.A. in 1934

been the standard for Western music for hundreds of years. Schoenberg's system is constituted of four series, termed 'prime', 'inversion', 'retrograde' and 'retrograde inversion'. Starling simply transferred an exemplary piece of music written according to this system to twelve rows of fluorescent strip lights that he had lowered from the gallery ceiling, effectively delineating a new space within the gallery. The lights flicker on and off, seemingly randomly, although clearly in progression from one side to the other, twelve-tone music made visible through that most fundamentally visual of means: light.

The lowered lights also serve to illuminate the other element of the piece, focussing on Schoenberg's 'machine' – a grand piano. The space is occupied by two pianos, one intact but in a state of disrepair, the other apparently in the process of being assembled from its various newly-formed constituent parts. On closer examination, however, there is something wrong with those parts – they are in fact inverted, the wrong way round, exact mirror-image replicas of the 'real' thing. The piano made from these elements would effectively transpose low notes to high and vice versa. *Inverted Retrograde Theme* therefore takes the structure of the space, the piano and Schoenberg's innovative method and integrates them, converting gallery to workshop, re-designing the piano to allow it to better suit part of Schoenberg's method and translating Schoenberg's system for the creation of sound into light.

CMYK / RGB 2001

Installation view, FRAC Languedoc-Roussillon, Montpellier

CMYK / RGB 2001

Details of installation view, FRAC Languedoc-Roussillon,
Montpellier

Inverted Retrograde Theme USA 2002

Installation view, Casey Kaplan,
New York

The Pink Museum, Porto 2001

Installation views (clockwise from top left):
Casa de Serralves, Rua de Serralves
Photographic studio, Rua Passos Manuel
Casa de Serralves, Rua de Serralves
Liga dos Combatentes, Rua da Alegeria

**Blue, Red, Green,
Yellow, Djungel** 2002

Installation views,
Dundee Contemporary Arts

A block-printed curtain based
on 'Aralia' designed c.1928 by
Josef Frank and produced
using 16 wood-blocks made
from a West Indian Cedar cut
in New Grant, Trinidad on
the 22nd March 2002.

 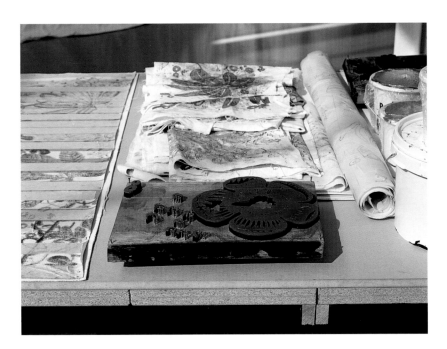

House for Weeds 2002

Installation view, Dundee
Contemporary Arts

A 1:3.5 scale model of the
Flower Kiosk, Malmö, Sweden,
designed in 1969 by Sigurd
Lewerentz.

The confluence of Starling's now apparent interest in a strand of 'organic modernism' developed largely in Scandinavia with his concern for the coercion of natural substances as backdrops to Western domesticity is the crux of *Djungel*, Starling's exhibition at DCA in June 2002. The exhibition presented three works: *Home-made Eames* (discussed above), *House for Weeds* and *Blue, Red, Green, Yellow, Djungel*, the two latter having been commissioned by DCA for the exhibition. The germs of the many strands that run through the two works are many, but the specific roots from which the *House for Weeds* grew lie in *Rescued Rhododendrons* (2000) a previous work that is nonetheless typical of Starling's careful approach to nature, one which Goethe would have been sure to acclaim. Invited to realise a public artwork for an outdoor sculpture project in Aberdeenshire, Starling chose to 'save' a number of rhododendron bushes that were due to be extracted from the site and destroyed. Rhododendrons, though they proliferate Scotland's country house gardens, are not indigenous, classed as weeds and have recently been the subject of much debate as to how to thwart their spread. The *rhododendron ponticum* species had been introduced to cultivation in Britain after it was discovered growing in the hills between Gibraltar and Cadiz in 1763 by a Swedish botanist named Claes Alstroemer, a student of Linnaeus.[12] Starling drove his small clutch of saved bushes, the descendents of Alstroemer's finds, in his old red (Swedish) car, from Aberdeenshire to Parque Los Alcornocales in southern Spain, reversing their ancestors' journey, returning the now unwanted goods to the place from whence they had come.

12. Carl Linneaus (Swedish, b.1707 – d.1778) known as the 'father of taxonomy'. Goethe claimed to have learned a lot from Linnaeus, but not botany.

The series of images taken at intervals on the journey through France and Spain shows an *ad hoc* studio set up, including Starling's car, the only clues to the specific locations in each instance being the quality of light and the character of the scenery behind them. These plants – the backdrop to many a country house in Scotland – become the stars, lit like models with the changing Western European landscape as their backdrop. *Rescued Rhododendrons* is a two-screen projected video installation that presents two sequences of still images that slowly fade into each other, some positive, some negative, refuting finality, refusing to identify a beginning or an end, but stressing rather the time and space of the process. It condenses over two hundred years of botanical history to ten minutes.

The beleaguered plants reappear in the immediate history of the *House for Weeds* (2002). Again invited to make a public work, this time for the new National Park (Scotland's first) around Loch Lomond.[13] Starling proposed building a house for the rhododendrons, a kind of sanctuary for the defunct and dispossessed plants. The house was to be an exact scale model of a flower kiosk designed in 1969 for the cemetery in Malmö, Sweden by Sigurd Lewerentz.[14] For various reasons the Loch Lomond project was not realised, but the architecture of the DCA gallery space was to prove the ideal grounds for a variation on the plan.

Lewerentz's original building, a prime example of simple modern, functionalism,

13. The Loch Lomond and The Trossachs National Park opened in July 2002. It covers 1,865 square kilometres. The Park's aims include the 'conservation and enhancement of the natural and cultural heritage of the area', as well as the promotion of its enjoyment. See *www.lochlomond-trossachs.org* for more information.

14. Sigurd Lewerentz (Swedish, b.1885 – d. 1975) architect active in the Swedish equivalent of the Arts & Crafts movement and best known for a number of churches designed in the 1920s.

Rescued Rhododendrons 2000

details from two-screen projected video
installation

features two sets of windows; one long, horizontal window giving onto the street and allowing passers-by to see the flowers and plants for sale, effectively the 'display' element of the function; and the other high up on the opposite (south-facing) wall, bringing as much light as possible into the kiosk, sustaining the 'growing' element of the function. Using discarded materials salvaged from waste around his studio, Starling constructed a 1: 3.5 scale model of the kiosk. The model was then hung high up on the gallery wall, striving, like a plant towards the daylight that streams through the gallery skylights. Starling's *House for Weeds* is, like the original building, organic in that it grows from and responds to its environment; it is opportunistic, seeking out the light and is comprised of unwanted materials, just like the rhododendrons and the eponymous weeds. It exists as a conduit between nature and society and succinctly expresses the function of display predicated on that commercialised relationship.

In contrast with the simple, legible, rational formalism of Lewerentz's building stands the bucolic floral flamboyance of Josef Frank's[15] remarkable textile designs, the starting point for *Blue, Red, Green, Yellow, Djungel* (2002). The piece is a typically diverse, loose but rich conglomeration that centres around Starling's labour-intensive re-production of Frank's '*Aralia*' print. His designs are just one of several strands that run through the work: the four-colour printing process of CMYK / RGB; the Vienna connection of *Inverted Retrograde Theme* that first led Starling to Frank. But the form taken by the final work makes explicit three of those strands, comprised as it is of three distinct elements. The first, in order of creation rather than appearance, a full West Indian Cedar tree, including its vast root-ball, brought from Trinidad, cut into sections and with part removed to create woodblocks for printing. The second, Starling's improvised printing table, eight metres long and comprised of a number of second-hand wooden tables adjusted to provide a uniform working surface. The third, a fifteen-metre wide linen curtain printed in part with a Frank design, which snakes its way between the gallery's supporting cast-iron pillars.

Designed by Frank in 1928, while still working in Vienna and one of around 170 designs he produced between 1919 and 1950, '*Aralia*' was, like all of Frank's designs, derived from secondary or even tertiary source material, such as children's book illustrations. For although tropical vegetation features in much of his work, Frank spent all his life in the city, first Vienna, briefly New York, but mostly Stockholm. He never visited the tropics, unlike Starling, who at the end of 2001 spent a month in Trinidad, where he made a series of photographs of a plantation of pine trees, which had been imported from Honduras in the 1970s. The plantation was an attempt to import commercial cultivation that proved unsuccessful, resulting in plots of non-indigenous species for which new uses have to be found. It abuts the real, authentic jungle.

15. Josef Frank (Austrian, b.1885 – d. 1967) designer associated with the Wiener Werkstätte, which, among other things, valued the work of the maker as much as that of the designer, and included the initials of both on the finished product. He settled in Sweden in 1934. Frank is said to have been influenced by the work of William Morris and his use of repeat pattern. For more on Frank see '*Josef Frank: Textile Designs*' by Kristina Wängberg-Eriksson (Bokförlaget Signum, Lund, 1999).

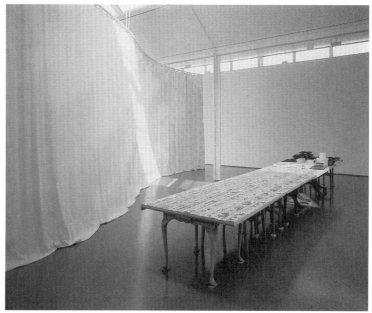

Blue, Red, Green, Yellow, Djungel 2002

Installation views, Dundee Contemporary Arts

left to right

Block printing of chintzes, 1912
in William Morris's workshop,
Merton Abbey (courtesy of the
William Morris Gallery, London)

Josef Frank master drawing for
'Vegetable Tree'
(photo Bruce White, courtesy of
Kristina Wängberg-Eriksson)

Josef Frank detail from master
drawing for 'Green Birds'.
(photo Tord Lund, courtesy of
Kristina Wängberg-Eriksson)

The jungle seems the inevitable place for Starling, a source of material, both physical and conceptual. The word itself conjures something of the morphological processes of meaning and place over time that feeds so much of his practice. Its definition indicates something of the spread from specific to general that he has often seemed keen to reverse:

1. *Equatorial forest area with luxuriant vegetation*
2. *Any dense or tangled thicket or growth*
3. *A place of intense or ruthless struggle for survival*

The tree brought from Trinidad provides an immediate tangible connection with the distant actual geographical source of Frank's design while the chosen print is truly a distilled and domesticated vision of some kind of dense and tangled growth. Even to the non-expert eye the design is clearly a fusion of elements that would never naturally co-exist. There are for example decidedly non-tropical oak leaves to be found running through the pattern.

That Frank should have finally produced the majority of his work in Sweden is symptomatic of one of the most significant aspects of 20th-century history to have shaped our physical environment: the mass emigration of intellectuals and 'creatives' like Schoenberg and Frank from Austria and Germany in the 1930s. Architects like Mies van der Rohe[16] found new and extensive opportunities in their chosen 'new world', particularly in the wealthy climate of post-war boom. The demographic shifts that occurred in the 1930s went a long way to enabling the spread of what was to become know as the International Style[17], which ironically though widely manifest in and associated with the US, originated in Europe – or more precisely in Europeans. The incredible ground-breaking design work that had been produced in the 1920s, with seminal, innovative projects such as Mies' 1929

16. Ludwig Mies van der Rohe
(German, b. Aachen 1886 –
d. Chicago 1969) architect,
furniture designer, and from
1930–33 the last director of
the Bauhaus, which he moved
to Berlin from its Gropius-
designed premises in Dessau.

17. The term 'International
Style' was first coined in 1931
by Alfred H. Barr, then
Director of the Museum of
Modern Art, New York.

18. The celebrated Pavilion was built as a temporary structure on Montjuic in Barcelona for the 1929 International Exhibition as the German Pavilion, in which King Alfonso XIII would be received by German authorities. The chairs were therefore designed as 'thrones' for the monarch. Demolished in 1930, it was later reconstructed on the original site, where it opened to the public in 1986.

19. Lilly Reich (German, b.1885 – d.1947) worked at the Wiener Werkstätte from 1908–11 and was head of interior design at the Bauhaus in its final years. She collaborated with Mies on many projects and is credited with designing, for example, many of the textiles that feature in some of his most famous works, including the buttoned calf-skin upholstery on the Barcelona chair. Cf. *'Lilly Reich: Designer and Architect'* by Matilda McQuaid, Museum of Modern Art, New York (1996)

Josef Frank detail from master drawing for 'Three Islands in the Black Sea' (photo Tord Lund, courtesy of Kristina Wängberg-Eriksson)

Barcelona Pavilion[18] and its furniture and Marcel Breuer's steel frame chairs of 1925, was the seed-bed of so much of what was to follow throughout the later part of the twentieth century. Significant among these achievements was a 1931 exhibition, *'The Dwelling in Our Time, German Building Exposition'* held in Berlin and co-directed by Mies with his regular collaborator, Lilly Reich.[19] Reich, who unlike many of her peers and friends remained in Berlin throughout the war, designed stunning structures and backdrops for the display of products, often introducing the process to the display.

The extent to which style infiltrated function in much of the Modernist project is perhaps best and most intriguingly evident in Mies' perhaps surprising predilection for curtains. Used to alter the atmosphere within his villas, they were sliding screens bringing

colour, texture and softness to the otherwise hard, cold surfaces of glass, steel and marble.[20] In a description of the infamous Farnsworth house in Illinois,[21] the usual eulogy of its pure form, as 'cubic simplicity with elegant precision of detail and immaculate finish in compositions of supreme poise and balance' continues somewhat surprisingly 'windows curtained in natural off-white shantung silk'. Silk, not cotton, linen or even wool and off-white too. Straying from a purely functional ethos, the joy of drapery must simply have proved too hard to resist.

With these stories in mind, Starling copied the design of 'Aralia' from a sample of the fabric, which is still in commercial production in Sweden, though using a different method than when first produced in 1928. Originally, it had been devised for wood-block printing and, like many of Frank and his peers' designs of the time, sought to re-invigorate what had been a dying technique with innovative pattern-making. Starling prepared sixteen drawings from the design, calculating the necessary colour separations and combinations. The drawings were then scanned into a computer that controlled the laser-cutting of the designs from sheets of timber cut from the Trinidadian tree.

20. Curtains were key elements in much of Mies' villa architecture, including the Barcelona Pavilion, which had a rich deep red curtain, and the much-lauded Tugendhat House at Brno in what is now the Czech Republic, commissioned by Fritz and Grete Tugendhat and built 1928-30. The latter included 'acid-green cowhide upholstery' on the sitting room furniture, designed by Reich.
21. Commissioned (1946) by a Dr Farnsworth, who, finding the finished house too expensive to live in, moved out and tried (unsuccessfully) to sue the architect. It is now well preserved as a private country retreat.

As well as being clearly hand-made, Starling's version of the print gradually breaks the pattern down into the four colours used, exposing the hidden structure of the pattern as well as allowing the creation of a clearing[22] in the jungle – for there is untreated white fabric at the centre of this curtain, the print having tailed off at either side of it, through the gradual elimination of each of the colours: first yellow, then green, red and finally blue.

In many ways and particularly to the more emotionally inclined viewer, *Blue Red Green Yellow Djungel* is Starling's homage to the extraordinary, progressive minds of individuals like Reich, Frank and Mies. It is also an acknowledgement of the cultural, economic and geo-political currents that shaped their work and where it was nurtured. In a pre-ecologically conscious world, it was of course tolerable for even liberal-minded customers to sanction the use of exquisite but expensive resources, such as onyx, marble, travertine and ebony in the making of their elegant, style-conscious homes.

Starling's work is full of such stories of geographic shifts, surprising origins, convoluted and unexpected developments with almost Marxist concepts to do with harnessing the means of production, devising and applying one's own labour, denying the essential mechanics of capitalism. But all of this occurs in work that provides not arid, conceptual document, but fundamentally visual, physical encounters that facilitate experiences, awareness and enjoyment of extraordinary people, places and moments in the histories of our material world. Starling betrays a fondness for those pioneers, while never losing sight of their flaws and co-existence with rampant capitalism. His process runs contrary to a romanticised looking to the past, but rather seeks to keep past, present and future equally charged, looking back to see how the future was envisioned and provided for. He takes the defunct and re-makes, remodels into a live inter-connection, a dia-chronic experience of co-dependence. At best it solicits an appreciation of difference, an empathy for known but not experienced distant sources. In tracking the transition of natural substances first to resources and subsequently to commodities, he shows us the complex origins of the backdrops of our domestic jungle.

22. According to Heidegger, the "clearing" is the space provided by art in which truth could 'set to work'. Cf. Martin Heidegger 'The Origin of the Work of Art' in *'Philosophies of Art and Beauty'* (New York, 1964)

Simon Starling

1967 Born Epsom
Lives and works in Glasgow

SOLO EXHIBITIONS

2002 *Kakteenhaus*, Portikus, Frankfurt
Museum of Contemporary Art, Sydney
Djungel, Dundee Contemporary Arts
Flaga (1972–2000), Galeria Franco Noero, Turin
Inverted Retrograde Theme USA, Casey Kaplan, New York

2001 *East Doors (North)*, Harris Museum & Art Gallery, Preston
Burn-Time, Lichthaus Plus Neue Kunst, Bremen, Germany (project)
Inverted Retrograde Theme, Secession, Vienna
Burn-Time, neugerriemschneider, Berlin
John Hansard Gallery, Southampton
Simon Starling / Poul Henningsen, Cooper Gallery, Duncan of Jordanstone College of Art and Design, Dundee
Simon Starling / Poul Henningsen, Kunstverein Hamburg
CMYK/RGB, FRAC Languedoc-Roussillon, Montpellier

2000 Camden Art Centre, London

1999 Signal, Malmö
Blinky Palermo Prize, Galerie für Zeitgenössische Kunst, Leipzig

1998 *Le Jardin suspendu*, The Modern Institute, Glasgow
Moderna Museet Project, Moderna Museet, Stockholm

1997 *Blue Boat Black*, Transmission Gallery, Glasgow

1995 The Showroom, London

SELECTED GROUP EXHIBITIONS

2002 *Zusammenhänge Herstellen*, Kunstverein Hamburg
Der Globale Komplex – Continental Drift, Grazer Kunstverein
Happy Outsiders, Zacheta Gallery, Warsaw and City Gallery of Contemporary Art, Katowice
My Head Is On Fire But My Heart Is Full Of Love, Charlottenborg, Copenhagen
Wrong Time, Wrong Place, Kunsthalle Basel

2001 *Words and Things*, CCA, Glasgow
Here + Now, Dundee Contemporary Arts, McManus Galleries, Dundee and Aberdeen Art Gallery
Total Object Complete With Missing Parts, Tramway, Glasgow
Squatters, Serralves Foundation, Porto
Silk Purse, Arnolfini, Bristol
Circles, ZKM, Karlsruhe

2000 *Play-Use*, Witte de Witt, Rotterdam
Open Country, Musée cantonal des Beaux-arts, Lausanne
Spacecraft, Bluecoat, Liverpool
Future Perfect, CVA, Cardiff
Artifice, Deste Foundation, Athens
What If/ Tänk om, Moderna Museet, Stockholm
Manifesta 3, Ljubljana
The British Art Show 5, Edinburgh, Cardiff and Southampton (touring)
Micropolitique, Le Magasin, Grenoble

1999   *Fireworks*, De Appel Foundation, Amsterdam

If I Ruled the World, The Living Art Museum, Reykjavik

Un Certain, ATA Centre d'Art Contemporain, Sofia

Dummy, Catalyst Arts, Belfast

Thinking Aloud, Kettle's Yard, Cambridge;
Cornerhouse, Manchester;
Camden Art Centre, London (touring)

1998   *Bad Faith*, 3 Month Gallery, Liverpool

Family, Inverleith House, Edinburgh

Strolling, Museum of Modern Art at Heide, Melbourne

1997   *L'Automne dans toutes ses collections*, MAC, Marseille

Nerve, ArtSpace, Sydney

Glasgow, Kunsthalle Bern, Kunsthalle Bern

B.c.c., Cleveland and The Tannery, London

1996   *Kilt ou Double*, La Vigie, Nîmes

Sick Building, Transmission Gallery at Globe Space, Copenhagen

City Limits, Staffordshire University, Stoke on Trent

1995   *Maikafer Flieg*, Bunker Köln-Ehrenfeld, Köln

Kabinett für Zeichnung Kampnagel, Hamburg

About Place, Collective Gallery, Edinburgh

1994   *Institute of Cultural Anxiety*, ICA, London

Oriel Mostyn Open, Oriel Mostyn, Llandudno

Modern Art, Transmission Gallery, Glasgow

Die Zweite Wirklichkeit, Aktuelle Aspekte des Mediums Kunst, Wilhelmspalais, Stuttgart

BT New Contemporaries, touring exhibition

Left Luggage, touring exhibition

1992   *Three New Works*, Transmission Gallery, Glasgow (with Paul Maguire)

Gesture No. 5, Post West Gallery, Adelaide

PUBLICATIONS

Simon Starling, Galerie für Zeitgenössische Kunst, Leipzig, 1999

Simon Starling, Moderna Museet, Stockholm, 1998

Back to Front, Camden Art Centre / John Hansard Gallery, 2001

Simon Starling / Poul Henningsen, Cooper Gallery, Duncan of Jordanstone College of Art and Design, Dundee, 2001

CMYK / RGB, FRAC Languedoc-Roussillon, Marseille, 2001

Simon Starling, Inverted Retrograde Theme, Secession, Vienna, 2001

Simon Starling · Djungel

Dundee Contemporary Arts
22 June – 11 August 2002

Supported by The Henry Moore Foundation

ISBN 0 95420260 0
Copyright © Simon Starling and
Dundee Contemporary Arts

All photography by Simon Starling except:
pp.32–33 Jens Elke; p.39 Erma Estiwck;
p.46 (left) Ruth Clark; p.54 William Morris Gallery.

Designed by Dalrymple
Printed by BAS Printers Ltd

Acknowledgments

Simon Starling would like to thank the following for their assistance and support in the production of *Djungel*: Henriette Bretton-Meyer; Katrina Brown; Scott Campbell; Garry Chin; Charlotte Elias; Paul Egan and Dougie Meldrum (Curtis Fine Papers, Ltd., Guardbridge, Fife); Glasgow Sculpture Studios; John Green; Simon Hopkins (Scott Associates, Glasgow); Susie Hunter; Iain Kettles; Sophie Macpherson; Andrew Miller; Donald Nesbitt (MNS Photocolour, Glasgow); Angus Nicoll (Peter Greig & Co Ltd., Kirkcaldy, Fife); Paragon Ensemble; Ralken Colours, Bradford; Andrea Re (Ferranti Photonics Ltd., Dundee); Svenskt Tenn, Stockholm; Paul Turnbull (block printers); Stephen Walker, PSK Marketing; Kristina Wängberg-Eriksson; Wasps Studios, Glasgow and Faith Liddell, Colin Lindsay, Rob Tufnell, Andrew Crichton, Scott Henriksen, Rob Hunter, Steve Lawrie, Derek Lodge and Campbell Sandilands at DCA.

Dundee Contemporary Arts

152 Nethergate · Dundee DD1 4DY
T +44 (0)1382 909900
F +44 (0)1382 909221
E dca@dundeecity.gov.uk
www.dca.org.uk

Director: Faith Liddell
Curator: Katrina Brown
Gallery Manager: Colin Lindsay
Assistant Curator: Rob Tufnell

At the front of the book

Paper production, Curtis Fine Papers, Guardbridge, Fife, Scotland, March 2002

At the back of the book

A house constructed using Honduran Pine trees planted in 1970 in place of the indigenous tropical vegetation on the hills overlooking Port of Spain, Trinidad, November 2001

Supported by